FAR AND AWAY
was produced and edited
by Imogen Bright and Vanessa Whinney

Text: Grace Polk
Design: S.M. Design
Artist: Francesca Pelizzoli

First published in Great Britain by
Eyebright Publications, 21 Weedon Lane,
Amersham, Bucks HP6 5QT, 1991

Copyright © Eyebright Publications, 1991

ISBN 0 948751 04 5

This book was set in Meridien by Tradespools, Frome
Printed and bound in Hong Kong

FAR AND AWAY

A Notebook for Travellers

CONTENTS

INTRODUCTION

The excitement of setting foot on a distant continent, the exhilaration of standing on the rim of the Grand Canyon, or just the peace of the French countryside as seen from a simple cottage – what you want or need from a vacation is entirely personal, and there are as many holidays as there are different people. For some it is the challenge, for others it is the enrichment of mind and spirit, while for many it is the change from the daily routine, which is important.

Whoever you are and wherever you go, you will surely wish to make the best of your trip and to enjoy it to the full. Holidays can be divided into three distinct phases, the ideas and the plans, the practical task of preparation, and the holiday itself. *Far and Away* has been designed with exactly these elements in mind. The book is intended to encompass the whole rich experience from the first idea to the distant memory, when you sit back in your armchair months or years later, and recall your adventures.

For some people holidays begin with dreams, while others are overwhelmed by the variety of choice. Does leafing through an atlas fill you with longings? Did that film evoke beautiful visions of a distant island? Use the first section, *The Holiday Dream*, to note your ideas and to create a memorable trip, whether you prefer an all inclusive package or wish to work out the details yourself. From your first dreams about faraway places to the careful study of esoteric travel guides, preparing a journey can be almost as absorbing as making the trip itself. This section is not intended to replace the host of excellent guides available. Rather, it will help you to bring together information which is most suited to your interests and needs – hotels, tourist offices, magnificent views, special dishes, local festivals.

Besides the dreaming and the information collecting, you will need to do some more mundane planning. The *Holiday Countdown* section has been included to help you keep track of the necessary practical preparations such as checking passports, getting the correct documents, and making an itinerary. It is useful to have a reminder of what to pack, and what to do before leaving home. At the end of the book there is a reference section, and the very last page is for you to fill in vital information which you might need in an unforeseen emergency.

Holidays were originally celebrations of religious festivals, and a time of release from everyday cares. The *Holiday Diary* is provided for you to make a unique record of your trip and its memories. Think of it as a letter to a close friend. It may lie in a drawer and be read with delight by your children ten or twenty years from now, or it may be the first chapter in the memoires of an inveterate traveller....you. Capture the first fleeting impressions, record a stimulating conversation, note the name of a wild flower, or praise a meal. If you're not keen on writing, try making some sketches or paste in mementos and photographs.

There are many ways to use *Far and Away*. If you do not devote the whole book to one major trip, you could divide the space between several vacations in one or more years. Alternatively, if you visit a particular place or country regularly, you might choose to keep it for those holidays only, so that you can compare the old and familiar with what is new, and end up with a fascinating notebook. If you travel with the family, they may wish to enter their thoughts at the end of the day.

Instead of keeping it as a personal and private record, you may prefer to share the completed volume with friends who can benefit from your research and re-live

your experiences. If you have a second home, you could keep the book there, filled with the names of the best restaurants, shops, sights, and useful local addresses. In this case, it could also become a guest book, with annotations and suggestions from your visitors. Ask everyone to be a restaurant critic, or to mention their favourite trip.

Although it is a beautiful book to treasure, it is small enough to carry around with you. Keep this book with you throughout your travels. As well as entering notes and impressions, you may encounter an emergency, and need to refer to the vital personal information which you filled in before leaving home. This is your book, make of it what you want. May these pages provide you with happy memories of grand experiences.

Bon Voyage!

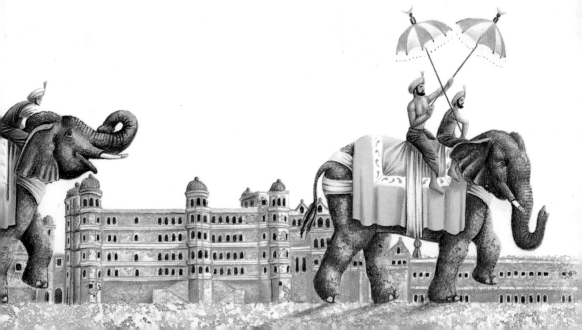

THE HOLIDAY DREAM

Having a dream and then setting out to make it come true – for many of us this is an ambition never realised, but in the case of holidays we can make an attempt, however humble. This section will prompt you to gather information to help you fulfil your highest aspirations.

Don't be afraid to let your fantasies run away with you, and invent the holiday of a lifetime. You may begin your entries months before you actually set off. In the comfort of your armchair, you may be inspired by an article or news item, a quote in a book, or a place on a map. Ideas which lead to grand tours may come from friends, television or radio. Jot these down on the *Ideas and Dreams* pages.

Then bring your dreams into focus. Enjoy finding out as much as possible about the pleasures of travel. Assemble the information you need about agents and ferry operators, have fun working out a spectacular route, note down sights to visit, delicious foods to sample or where to go for the best fishing or to make the most advantageous purchases. Once the trip begins, feel free to expand the lists and ideas.

Although you are sure to write about specific places in the *Holiday Diary* section, this *Holiday Dream* section will be useful for quick reference once your trip is over. Instead of being buried in the *Diary*, addresses, telephone numbers and opening times will be easier to find here. Think of those who follow in your footsteps (friends who may wish to borrow this book) or of your own return visit, and enter the best beaches, names of chefs, modify shop and museum opening hours, star the favourite sights you saw. Even note the places you wish to avoid in the future!

Ideas and Dreams

_____
_____
_____
_____
_____
_____
_____
_____
_____
_____
_____
_____
_____
_____
_____
_____

Holidays begin with dreams – dreams unhampered by
monetary constraints or transportation cares. Visions of an
Aegean island captured by a great photographer, paintings
of an exotic South Pacific paradise, reports of a Himalayan
conquest, any of these may set your imagination whirring.

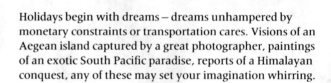

_____

_____

_____

_____

_____

_____

_____

_____

_____

_____

_____

_____

_____

Did that adventure story make you want to visit Turkey or
the diaries of a Victorian traveller excite your curiosity about
Samarkand? Does leafing through an atlas fill you with
longings? Do articles in the Sunday paper set your mind
racing around the globe? Then put your pen to these pages,
write down your dreams, and keep articles and references of
particular interest.

Ideas and Dreams

_____

_____

_____

_____

_____

_____

_____

_____

_____

_____

_____

_____

_____

_____

_____

Try a new holiday idea next year. Experience hot air ballooning, volunteer on an archeological dig, master Italian cooking in Parma or pick grapes in France. Visit landmarks in the life of your favourite rock star or writer, focus on the art and architecture of a specific period, specialise in theme parks or gorgeous gardens. There are even special battlefield tours available.

_____

_____

_____

_____

_____

_____

_____

_____

_____

_____

_____

_____

Fill these pages with ideas, names of countries, types of holiday, whatever you like. Perhaps you'll start by making a personal profile, to gauge your individual fitness for certain holidays. What is your favourite climate, do you like leisurely or physically demanding holidays, do you prefer the peace of the countryside or noise of a city? Adapt the dream holiday to the realities of your lifestyle.

Travel Agents and Tour Operators

_____

_____

_____

_____

_____

_____

_____

_____

_____

_____

_____

In order to realise your ideas and dreams, you need to obtain expert advice for both independent and package holidays. Be it a bicycle tour, a weekend city break or a white water rafting experience, find the best experts for your purposes, and note the names here. The national tourist office of the country you plan to visit is a great resource for appropriate travel agents as well as brochures and maps.

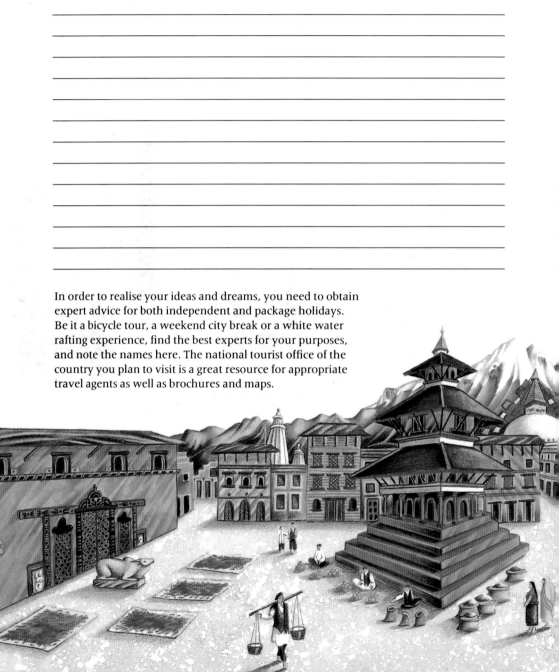

_____

_____

_____

_____

_____

_____

_____

_____

_____

_____

_____

_____

_____

A travel agent sells tickets and package tours, books hotels and cruises, and should be able to design a personal itinerary. Most package tours are prepared by specialist tour operators. Use these pages to note names, numbers and specialities – the African photo safari packager may not be best for an organised ski holiday. A travel agent who books student treks in Nepal may not be current on luxury Amazon cruises for the retired.

Travel Agents and Tour Operators

_____
_____
_____
_____
_____
_____
_____
_____
_____
_____

Reliability and an established reputation are very important
in choosing a tour operator or agent. Either can easily go
bankrupt, but the reputable ones have professional
organisations which protect their clients. Unadvertised
discount fares are frequently available on regular airlines to
their biggest agency customers. Find a travel agent who
takes advantage of block airline bookings, and always
compare prices.

If you are planning that holiday of a lifetime, you may wish to spend several years making your plans. It may not cost you all that much extra to go all the way round the world. There are specialist agencies who can offer advice on different permutations.

Planning the Route

Working out a route and all the things you want to see is
endlessly absorbing, and open to variations and additions.
This is where you can experiment with a variety of possible
itineraries fitting in all the highlights. Aficionados of travel
on water may prefer a Danube cruise to reach Vienna, or a
sea voyage to reach Stockholm, Helsinki or Leningrad. Train
buffs may be inspired by restored luxury train routes in
Scotland or Spain.

When you are reading about your destination, you are sure to come across descriptions of wonderful views and breath-taking sights that you won't want to miss, whether driving, cycling or walking. Some maps highlight picturesque routes that are worth a detour. Allow plenty of time to enjoy these at leisure. Automobile associations provide members with personal route planning services, and can alert you to detours, avalanche closings, difficult mountain passes and washed out roads.

Planning the Route

When making your plane reservation for a long flight, enquire about special meals available: low salt, low calorie, vegetarian, Kosher, fish and children's menus are some alternatives. First time travellers, handicapped and elderly passengers should ask their travel or ticket agent for special assistance at airports and with connections. Customer service agents are glad to provide wheelchairs or electric carts, if advised ahead of arrival time.

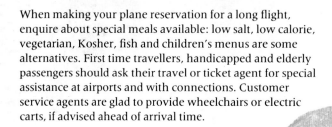

_____

_____

_____

_____

_____

_____

_____

_____

_____

_____

_____

You can avoid being bumped from an overbooked flight by arriving at the check-in in plenty of time. If you are willing to be 'pulled' from a full flight, the airline may reward you with a free ticket anywhere on their route, *and* a seat on the next available flight. If mechanical delays cause you to miss a plane connection, a reasonable carrier should take care of you. This could mean a free meal or hotel room, or a flight on another carrier. Airlines are not so generous when delays are caused by bad weather.

Getting Around

Elephants, camels, llamas and rickshaws provide the
traveller with exotic memories that long outlive
recollections of shuttle planes and car ferries. Getting to a
destination should be efficient, worry-free, and comfortable:
need one ask for more? To ensure a smooth journey, begin
by exploring possible means of transport on these pages.

National railways, in Holland and Germany for example, offer very reasonable multiple day passes to anyone who purchases their ticket *before* going abroad. Brazil and the United States offer comparable airplane passes. All senior citizens are entitled to purchase the French Carte Vermeil for discounts on the national railway. Compare schedules, rates and special deals, and note them here.

Travel by Car

If you intend to drive in a foreign country, find out about special regulations and different driving habits, and keep the information here. Ask your insurance company and automobile association if you need any special documents when travelling abroad. Photocopy car documents and carry them separately. This could save problems should you lose the originals. If you are taking your own car on holiday, use the check list on page 58.

_____

_____

_____

_____

_____

_____

_____

_____

_____

_____

_____

Before driving off in a hired car, check that the following are provided: emergency equipment including a reflective triangle, new spare tyre, good working windscreen wipers, and operator's manual. Make sure the tyres are in good condition, and that the petrol tank is full. Ask hotels to send you a map of their city indicating their location in advance. If driving alone, it will help you to check on the correct highway exit or approach from the town centre.

Where to Stay

Here is a place to put down the names, addresses and
comments that friends have shared with you: camp sites,
hotels, or villas to rent. Note agencies for self- catering
holidays, gites, home exchanges. Keep suggestions from
guide books and ideas from newspapers. Transfer finalized
arrangements to the itinerary on page 68.

_____
_____
_____
_____
_____
_____
_____
_____
_____
_____
_____
_____
_____
_____
_____

Lovely hotel, noisy room? If you arrive in the afternoon, ask the management to show you alternatives. Be absolutely specific: sunny, view, terrace, away from garbage collection (invariably at 5.00 a.m.), away from the housekeeper's room, not facing a construction site or alongside an archaic lift. You may have to decide which is most important to you – good facilities or a splendid view of the River Arno.

Where to Stay

Smaller or older hotels, often run by families, may be just right for your next visit. Always keep notes of possible hotels for future trips. You never know when they might be useful. Choose a quiet time after check-out time, and ask to see some of their rooms. If you want to stay in a Parador or Pousada in Spain or Portugal, with their beautiful settings and high quality service, you are advised to book at least six months in advance.

_____

_____

_____

_____

_____

_____

_____

_____

_____

_____

Traditional Japanese inns, or ryokans, are a spartan but reasonable alternative to the big international hotels. Here you can experience the native lifestyle, sleep on a futon, and meditate in the serene gardens. Climb into a deep hot tub for a relaxing soak, after washing and rinsing of course. Your room maid will hand you a robe, and tell you exactly what to do during your stay.

Eating and Drinking

_____
_____
_____
_____
_____
_____
_____
_____
_____
_____
_____
_____
_____
_____
_____

Instead of dragging along still another guide book, jot down
the five star places you've read about, and that friends have
swooned over. Make a note of the speciality of the house
and the best wines. After your trip is over, record your own
finds here, with addresses. Better still, save the menu to
share with others.

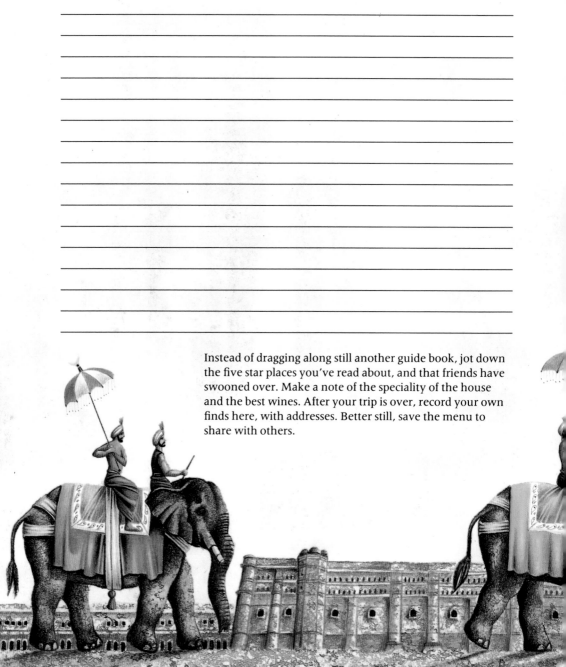

_____

_____

_____

_____

_____

_____

_____

_____

_____

_____

_____

_____

_____

Was your dinner divine? Keep the name of the chef, and if you wish to avoid disappointment, check that he is there before you go back. He's sure to have a night off, and your meal may be too. If he moves to another restaurant, he'll be flattered that you've followed him.

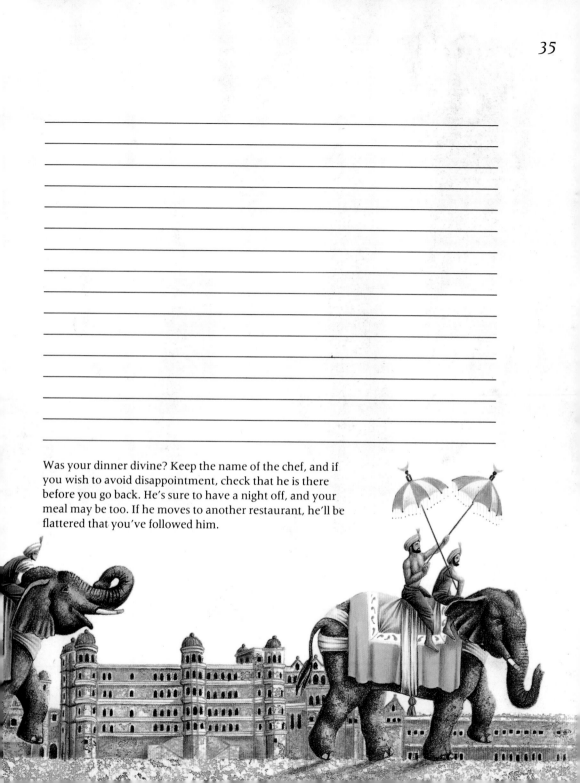

Eating and Drinking

_____

_____

_____

_____

_____

_____

_____

_____

_____

_____

_____

_____

Muffins, cinnamon rolls, bagels, the choice in the US is mouth watering. In Russia, ice cream and caviar are the about the only foods to be recommended. Try to find out about national dishes so that you can be adventurous in your eating while you are on holiday, even if it is only a matter of enjoying a local fish or cheese.

_____

_____

_____

_____

_____

_____

_____

_____

_____

_____

_____

_____

_____

_____

_____

_____

_____

_____

Brazilian fejoada, Danish smorgasbord, Nepalese curry,
Moroccan couscous or bastilla are as much a cultural
experience as a culinary one. Local specialities will
invariably be better than nondescript 'international'
preparations or efforts to imitate your personal favourites.
The Iranians, Indians and Turks make much more
interesting hamburgers than Americans do. Instead of a
hotel brunch, share a table with locals for dim sum in Hong
Kong or during an Italian festa.

Things to Do and See

_____
_____
_____
_____
_____
_____
_____
_____
_____
_____
_____
_____

Start making notes of the local sights to visit when you get to
your destination. Ask previous visitors what they would
recommend. The local tourist office abroad will provide you
with specifics about the village or area, and even make hotel
or guest house reservations for you. You can write directly to
the Office of Tourism in any town in France or Austria for a
bundle of information. Follow the 'i' sign at most train
stations in Europe, and you'll find an English-speaking
person to assist you.

_____

_____

_____

_____

_____

_____

_____

_____

_____

_____

_____

_____

_____

_____

_____

_____

_____

Even the most careful pre-planner may find certain sights temporarily closed or swathed in scaffolding. Don't go miles out of your way without calling ahead to make sure the place you *must* see is open, especially if it is during the Christmas season, Ramadan, Holy Week or holiday time.

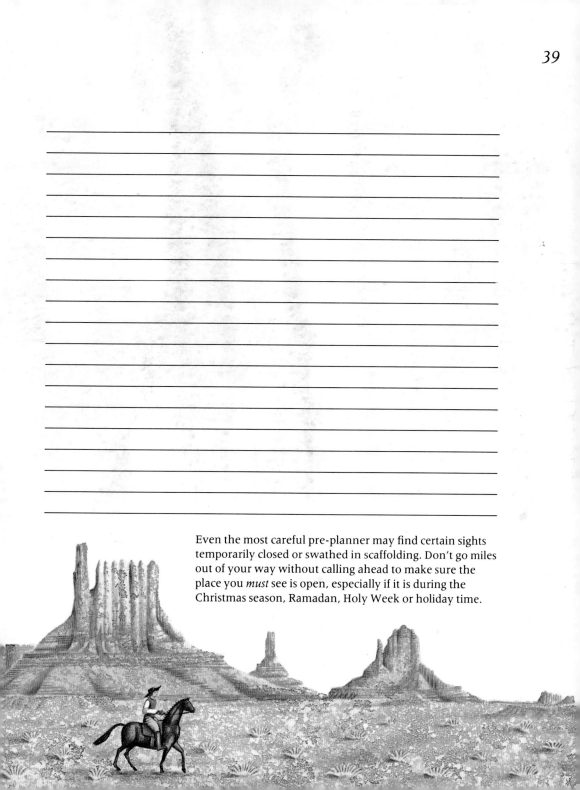

Things to Do and See

_____

_____

_____

_____

_____

_____

_____

_____

_____

_____

_____

_____

_____

If you crave fresh air, note possibilities for enjoying your favourite activities – riding, fishing, hiking or jogging, biking or tennis. If you plan to go to the theatre, opera or any special events, collect the names of local ticket agencies. When you get to your destination, try to buy magazines listing the week's events. Some European cities publish English language newspapers.

_____

_____

_____

_____

_____

_____

_____

_____

_____

_____

_____

_____

_____

_____

Focus in on places to see, and things to do that must be part of your holiday – children's zoos, coral reefs, national parks, stately homes, ancient ruins, special museum exhibitions, musical events and local festivals. Big festivals generate crowds; either be part of them or don't go anywhere near them. See the list of festivals on page 152.

Shopping

_____

_____

_____

_____

_____

_____

_____

_____

_____

_____

Scribble in the day of the week to catch the flea or special food market, the location of the discount designer shops (Rue d'Aboukir in Paris or Loehmann's in New York), the local craft speciality, the custom tailor in Hong Kong, if not before you get to your destination, then once you're there. You'll certainly be passing on these addresses to your friends. Note the prices you paid for Florentine gold, Portuguese ceramics, Ecuadorian rugs and Panama hats.

You may qualify for up to a twenty per cent VAT refund in the EC and some other countries. Request a refund form when you make large purchases, preferably using a credit card to simplify obtaining the refund. When you leave the country, show the unused product to customs and have the form stamped. Keep the receipt, and mail the form back to the shop where you made your purchases. Allow about two months for the refund to arrive.

Friends to Visit

_____
_____
_____
_____
_____
_____
_____
_____
_____
_____
_____
_____
_____
_____

Friends or friends of friends may be yachting in Capri, or living near Disneyland. Your distant relatives in Auckland want to hear from you 'when you arrive'. Their names and numbers belong here. Be sure to look them up, as getting to know the locals always adds immeasurably to a holiday. But don't overstay your welcome!

Writing Home

_____
_____
_____
_____
_____
_____
_____
_____
_____
_____
_____
_____
_____
_____
_____
_____
_____
_____
_____
_____
_____
_____

Birthday cards and gifts are more exciting when sent
from abroad. Don't forget to jot down the names and
addresses of those to whom you promised to send a postcard. or who love the place you are visiting. Or use these
pages for a gift list for those back home.

_____

_____

_____

_____

_____

_____

_____

_____

_____

_____

_____

_____

For the really keen correspondent, pre-addressed, self- stick labels are as common now as the xeroxed Christmas letter. They save you taking a heavy address book with you, and make postcard addressing en masse quicker and simpler. Xeroxed labels will last you for more than one trip. If you eschew lengthy prose, postal rates in certain countries are cheaper for cards with a five-word message.

Traveller's Library

_____
_____
_____
_____
_____
_____
_____
_____
_____
_____
_____
_____
_____
_____
_____
_____

Novels, essays, volumes have been written about places you
have dreamed about. Here's a place to jot down those you
want to read, the best guide book to look for, as well as
recommendations of friends. Don't overlook the works of J.
Morris, V.S. Naipaul, Paul Theroux, E.M. Forster, H.V.
Morton or the classics of other eras which convey flavour
and atmosphere. Old guides books are inspiring to read,
even if maps and prices are out of date.

49

_____
_____
_____
_____
_____
_____
_____
_____
_____
_____
_____
_____
_____
_____
_____
_____
_____
_____
_____

Holiday books fall into three categories: guide books, travel books, and light reading. Air travel in particular calls for light reading – in weight and substance. Don't load yourself down with anything profound for your flight. List books to read when you get home too, and perhaps collect some specially vivid quotations which strike you.

HOLIDAY COUNTDOWN

Seasoned travellers have found that careful vacation planning helps to prevent unpleasant surprises, but still allows for spontaneous discoveries. This section is intended to take the stress out of a trip, and to avoid last minute panics.

While you are still developing your dreams, you may wish to start listing a few checks and reminders – your passport, booking dates, pre-trip shopping and so on. In this way you can keep track of the practical side of the holiday. Start by making sure that you can afford to realise your dream, and end up with a planned itinerary to use as you set off at the start of the holiday itself.

Even if you find that planning cramps your style, be sure to complete the page of *Vital Information* at the end of the book (page 160), which may help you in an emergency. If there is not enough space for your own particular planning needs, just use the blank pages of the *Holiday Diary* – this is your notebook after all.

Costing the Dream

Before you get too carried away, work out how much you
can afford to spend on your holiday. Did you overspend last
time? Would it be cheaper to take a package holiday or to
make your own arrangements? Use this page to work out
your overall budget, and also to estimate your daily living
expenses such as food, hotels, petrol. Are there any
restrictions on taking money in and out of the country your
are visiting? What are the current exchange rates? Keep
helpful notes on the opposite page.

	PRE-PAID	ESTIMATE	ACTUAL
PACKAGE TOUR			
HOTEL DEPOSITS			
FARES			
TRANSPORT			
PETROL			
ACCOMMODATION			
FOOD AND DRINK			
ENTERTAINMENT			
GIFTS			
OTHER			
TOTAL			

When you have done your overall calculations, you will
need to decide in what form to take your money. Do you
prefer to take most of it as travellers cheques or currency, or
will you rely on credit cards? Card companies can give useful
information about using your card, and whether you can
use it to draw cash. Your bank can tell you whether, and
where, you can draw cash using your cash card. After your
trip, work out what you have actually spent. Don't forget to
save receipts for possible tax deductions.

TYPE OF MONEY	TAKEN	RETURNED	FINAL EXPENDITURE
TRAVELLERS CHEQUES			
CURRENCIES: OWN			
FOREIGN			
CREDIT CARD BILLS			
TOTAL			

NOTES:

Countdown 1

Last minute anxieties can be averted by establishing
deadlines for yourself. Start with the earliest necessary
preparation date, and then tick off when you have dealt with
each item. Allow plenty of time for obtaining passports and
visas, especially during peak travel months. Make certain
that credit cards and driving licenses don't expire while you
are away. It may be wise to get a separate passport for an
infant. If you are taking your car, see page 60. You can
prepare a shopping list on page 62. Start arranging for home
security well in advance by asking a neighbour to be
watchful in your absence. Hire someone to cut the grass,
rake the leaves, water the windowboxes or to care for
houseplants. Cancel deliveries in good time.

THREE MONTHS BEFORE DEPARTURE

TWO MONTHS BEFORE DEPARTURE

ONE MONTH BEFORE DEPARTURE

_____

_____

_____

_____

_____

_____

_____

SECURING YOUR HOME 1

MILK

PAPERS

MAIL

OTHER DELIVERIES

_____

_____

KEY

NEIGHBOURS

POLICE

ANIMALS

GARDEN

HOUSEPLANTS

CAR

_____

_____

_____

Countdown 2

Some people find it helpful to have a separate list for the last
few days before departure, including the very last day. The
police recommend putting time switch plugs on your lights,
both upstairs and down. Bills may arrive in your absence, so
if you can anticipate certain payments you may avoid
problems on your return. When you have made all the main
preparations, go round your home checking all the security
points. Finally, as you actually leave home, check you have
tickets, money and passport. Your itinerary should be clearly
set out on page 68 of this book.

LAST FEW DAYS

_____
_____
_____
_____
_____
_____
_____
_____

LAST DAY

_____
_____
_____
_____
_____
_____
_____
_____
_____
_____

SECURING YOUR HOME 2

TELEPHONE/ANSWERING MACHINE

TIME SWITCHES

ELECTRICITY

WATER

GAS

HEATING

TELEVISION

VIDEO

BURGLAR ALARM

WINDOWS

DOORS

OTHER

AS YOU LEAVE

TRAVEL DOCUMENTS

TICKETS

PASSPORT AND VISA

MONEY

HEALTH CARD

INSURANCE

MEDICINES

HOUSE KEY

OTHER

Healthy Travel

Here's the place to list all the steps you need to take to
ensure a healthy holiday. If you are going on a long journey
or your holiday will involve a major climate change or
unusual exertion, have a full check up. Information on
inoculations is available from your national department of
health. Your first aid kit may be simple or complex, with
prescriptions, vitamins or tropical medications, depending
on your destination. Make your own list, and if necessary
consult a doctor.

INOCULATIONS

_____

_____

_____

_____

_____

_____

MEDICAL CHECK UPS

_____

_____

_____

_____

_____

_____

HEALTH INSURANCE

_____

_____

_____

_____

_____

_____

FIRST AID KIT

_____

_____

_____

_____

_____

_____

_____

_____

_____

_____

_____

_____

_____

_____

PRESCRIPTIONS/REMEDIES

_____

_____

_____

_____

_____

_____

_____

_____

_____

_____

_____

_____

Vehicle Checklist

Before leaving for a long journey, have your car looked over
thoroughly, including lights, brakes, tyres and wheel
alignment, oil and oil filter, bearing in mind the climate you
will encounter. Make a checklist of items that you usually
need such as pillows, maps, flashlight or snow chains. Keep
a copy of your car documents in a separate place in case of
theft. If you are trailing a boat or a caravan, remember to
check the connections and lights, and don't be tempted to
speed on motorways.

Pre-Trip Shopping

Does every member of the family have the necessary
wardrobe and personal items for the forthcoming trip? Note
here any special attire, pharmaceuticals, equipment, gifts or
films that you need to get before you leave, and tick them off
as you buy them. Don't rely on being able to find your
favourite toothpaste or cough pastels when you get to your
destination.

Packing List 1

Quarrelsome couples should carry separate pieces of
luggage, and keep separate lists of what they are each taking
so that they can't blame the other for forgetting anything.
This should be a peaceful trip! Everyone has their own
special needs when travelling: soft sponge ear plugs,
eyeshades, an extra pair of sunglasses, binoculars, beach
towel, Swiss army knife, torch or inflatable hangers. A
selection of plastic bags will always come in useful. Make
your own list of indispensables.

Packing List 2

Children have special needs. Use this page for making a
packing list for them, or else reserve it for your own special
vacations: winter sports, sailing holiday, or self-catering
holidays when you need to take food, sheets, or extensive
equipment.

Itinerary

This is your intended itinerary, with departure times, confirmation numbers for ticket and ferry reservations, accommodation addresses and telephone numbers as well as connecting times for trains and planes. It would be useful to put the ribbon marker on this page for easy reference while you are en route.

Itinerary

Here are some extra pages for your itinerary, and to keep any notes you may need to refer to while travelling. The secluded villa or country cottage you rented could be a nightmare to find. Get detailed instructions and a map, and plan to arrive in daylight. Note a telephone contact who can give you instructions from the nearest town.

HOLIDAY DIARY

A journal is as individual as the person keeping it, whether simple notes or florid descriptions. It does not have to be a boring daily log. While you may want to record the weather, the day's budget, or the long wait for the clouds to lift off the peak of Mont Blanc, don't forget your first impressions of great monuments or fabled palaces. Include your feelings: elation or exasperation, amazement or confusion, wonder or delight. Above all, let your imagination and creativity flow in this section.

Jot down comments from local guides that make a place come alive. Make notes of what makes you laugh: an anecdote or descriptive phrase. Include foreign expressions that the books neglect to mention, or that paved the way to a great experience. Describe the people you meet. Guidebooks may conjure up the places you visited, but they can't depict the family with whom you shared your compartment, or regale you with tall tales told by a fellow hitchhiker.

Pull out the book while sitting in a cafe, and note the details of the scene going on around you. If you're travelling with family or friends, let each member make their own entries or include their opinions. If blank paper frightens you, design your own formula to include what matters to you, for example weather, route, restaurants, wildlife observed, subjects painted or photographed, sights visited, mountains climbed or challenges encountered. Perhaps leave some blank pages for postcards, photographs, tickets or sketches.

Once you're back home, you may wish to evaluate your trip. Were your expectations fulfilled? What were the best aspects of the vacation? What would you change if you were to do it over again? Where would you like to spend more time? Special names or information can be transferred to The *Holiday Dream* section.

Wedding packages provide everything for getting married in paradise – the ceremony, the marriage licence and certificate, cake, food, champagne, the photographer as well as heavenly accomodation. All you need to do is to find your spouse.

_____

_____

_____

_____

_____

_____

_____

_____

_____

_____

_____

_____

_____

_____

_____

_____

_____

_____

_____

Vegetarian cruises, environmental trips or exploring the
wild life of northern Spain – whenever you hear of a
specialist tour operator or a good travel idea, note it down
on the *Ideas and Dreams* page.

Good timing can make all the difference to your enjoyment
and your memories of a wonderful holiday. You need to get
to the top of Mount Kilimanjaro before it clouds over in mid
morning. Take an early morning plane trip to the Grand
Canyon before the going gets bumpy. Visit the temples of
Angkor Wat by moonlight.

To counter jet lag and dehydration on long flights, airline crews recommend drinking a cup of still water for every hour aloft. Avoid drinks containing caffeine or alcohol, as they dehydrate you further. Wear glasses rather than contact lenses. Make liberal use of eye drops, moisturizer and hand lotion.

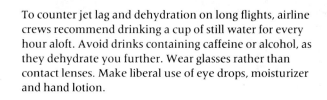

_____

_____

_____

_____

_____

_____

_____

_____

_____

_____

_____

_____

_____

_____

_____

Pick up business cards from rural taxi companies. Note the name of the driver/owner and his rates with your Vital Information on page 160.

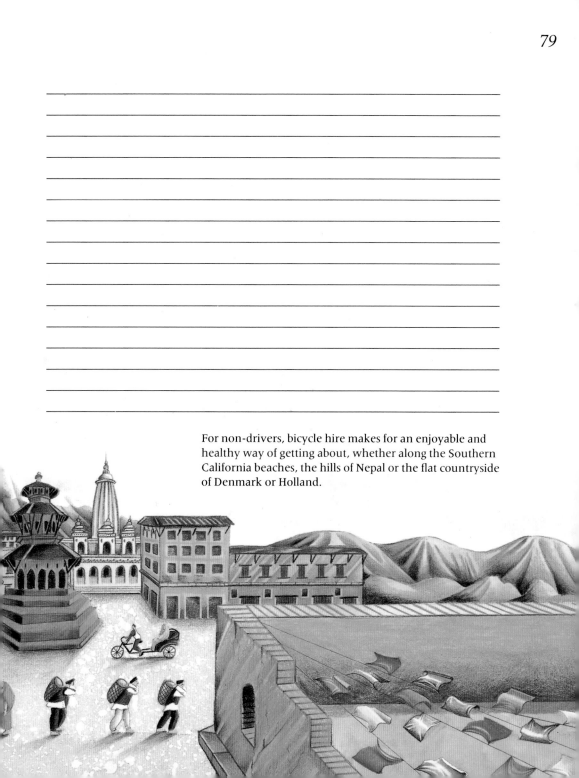

For non-drivers, bicycle hire makes for an enjoyable and healthy way of getting about, whether along the Southern California beaches, the hills of Nepal or the flat countryside of Denmark or Holland.

_____

_____

_____

_____

_____

_____

_____

_____

_____

_____

If you are a woman and you wish to travel alone, go ahead.
Don't be talked out of it. You should enjoy being by yourself,
so that you can treasure your moments of solitude. Choose
your destination wisely: a romantic place with honey-
mooners would be depressing. Plan evening activities to take
advantage of cultural or sporting events. Seek out
restaurants where everyone sits at communal tables.

In third world countries, it is advisable for a woman travelling on her own to take single or multiple-day trips with local tour operators. Women will be uncomfortable travelling alone in Muslim countries such as Pakistan, whereas in China they are perfectly safe. Don't look an Asiatic in the eye, unless you wish him to make you supremely happy!

82

_____
_____
_____
_____
_____
_____
_____
_____
_____
_____
_____
_____
_____
_____
_____
_____

A popular game when you are travelling with children is
I-Spy, or else try the game which begins 'My Aunt went to
Paris and put in her suitcase...'. Each person has to
remember what the previous person has listed and then add
a new item to the list.

_____
_____
_____
_____
_____
_____
_____
_____
_____
_____
_____
_____
_____
_____
_____

Other time fillers are small puzzles, colouring and puzzle books, travel chess and ludo. Tapes of favourite stories or music on a Walkman also provide entertainment during dull moments.

In Malawi, women may not wear dresses above the knee, shorts or trousers, while men cannot enter the country with long hair or flaired trousers! Modesty in dress (nothing sleeveless) is a safe rule in Muslim countries, Africa, India, China and in catholic churches.

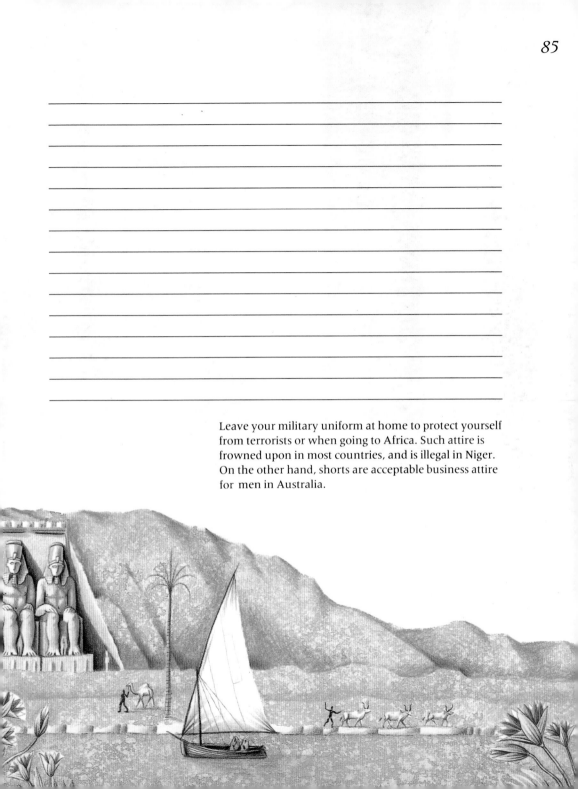

Leave your military uniform at home to protect yourself from terrorists or when going to Africa. Such attire is frowned upon in most countries, and is illegal in Niger. On the other hand, shorts are acceptable business attire for men in Australia.

In some countries and small towns, credit cards are not readily accepted. Germans prefer Eurocheques, and the French are more accustomed to their bank cheques.

Unless the currency is restricted, it's wise to carry some small change with you when you enter a country. You may need it for train tickets, phone calls or for tipping the hotel porter.

It is worth making a note of how long journeys take – whether by air, train or car. The more information you record, the more vivid your memory will be, and the more useful it will be for your friends reading your journal.

_____
_____
_____
_____
_____
_____
_____
_____
_____
_____
_____
_____
_____
_____
_____

Children will enjoy the 'legs' game when motoring through
the countryside. Each passenger takes turns spotting a pub
sign, and gets credit for the number of legs on that sign. On
motorways, see who can make the longest word incorpor-
ating the letters on passing number plates in correct order.

_____
_____
_____
_____
_____
_____
_____
_____
_____
_____
_____
_____
_____
_____
_____
_____
_____
_____
_____

The cost conscious will want to keep a record of daily expenses. At the end of the holiday check the totals against your original budget on page 52. Some people find it worth while to record exchange rates too, and banks where exchange rates are most advantageous.

_____
_____
_____
_____
_____
_____
_____
_____
_____
_____
_____
_____
_____
_____
_____
_____
_____
_____
_____

Credit card purchases made abroad may take over a month to appear on your statement, thus providing useful interest-free credit. Of course the rate of exchange may well have fluctuated in that time, so be prepared for surprises, pleasant or otherwise.

_____

_____

_____

_____

_____

_____

_____

_____

_____

_____

_____

Being left-handed can be a hazard in some countries. In most of South East Asia, Africa and the Middle East, never present a business card with your left hand. In Japan, present your card, with all your titles, with both hands. Never use your left hand to touch food when eating in an Arab country.

It's hard to get a straight answer from the Japanese. They will never say 'no' in public. The closest they come is to say sadly 'it is difficult'. Beware of the spoken affirmative, which may not mean 'yes'. It can simply be a reluctance to disappoint, as in 'I see', or 'I understand'.

In third world countries, avoid dysentery-causing foods: uncooked vegetables and salads, unpeeled fruit, unboiled water, milk and ice cubes, hard-boiled eggs, and cold meats. Use bottled or boiled water when cleaning your teeth.

_____

_____

_____

_____

_____

_____

_____

_____

_____

_____

_____

_____

_____

_____

Take a separate bag on any long journey, with your favourite fruit, snack or bottle of water to offset the vagaries of catering. Then you won't have to scramble about digging these items out of different bags or cases.

_____

_____

_____

_____

_____

_____

_____

_____

_____

_____

_____

_____

_____

_____

_____

_____

When obtaining hotel rates, check to see if they include breakfast and taxes. In many countries, breakfast at the hotel may entail an excessive separate charge. Savvy travellers in big-city American hotels save time and money by breakfasting in coffee shops nearby.

There's no VAT in the US, but there is a sales tax, which varies from state to state. Some states add an old age tax or entertainment tax as well. To confuse matters further, the hotel and occupancy tax has nothing to do with the sales tax. Restaurant bills rarely include a service charge.

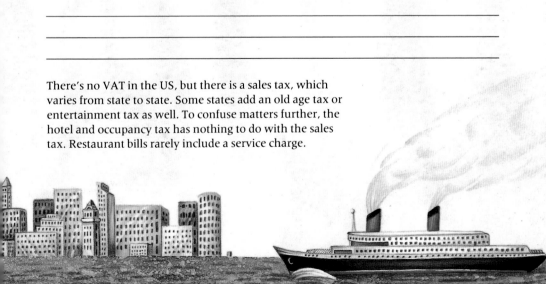

_____

_____

_____

_____

_____

_____

_____

_____

_____

_____

_____

_____

_____

_____

_____

Take plenty of your favourite film with you. It's invariably more expensive abroad, if available at all. Don't put your camera or film in the car glove compartment where it can get very hot in summer. Don't put film in your checked-in luggage; carry it with you.

Dress for long plane journeys in loose fitting clothes. For in-flight napping bring along ear plugs, eye shades, socks and a long sleeved sweater. Wear slippers in flight, and take shoes that will accommodate swollen feet when you arrive at your trip's end.

_____
_____
_____
_____
_____
_____
_____
_____
_____
_____
_____
_____
_____
_____
_____
_____

Most first time visitors to Australia will want to see as much as possible. The country has more unique features, flora and fauna than any other in the world. Others may prefer to concentrate on one area, for example the island of Tasmania with its rugged mountains, good fishing and yachting, and uncrowded beaches. The Outback, with Alice Springs as a base would fill another vacation, and the west coast around Perth a third.

_____

_____

_____

_____

_____

_____

_____

_____

_____

_____

_____

_____

In countries such as Thailand or Morocco, where bargaining is the norm, prices may be marked 100-300 per cent higher than the seller is willing to accept after serious haggling. Expect to drink many cups of mint tea while shopping for a carpet in Tunisia; the process is lengthy. Similarly, in South America, merchants weigh your offer in a leisurely manner over strong coffee.

_____
_____
_____
_____
_____
_____
_____
_____
_____
_____
_____
_____

Bangkok and Hong Kong are known for 24-hour dress-maker and tailor service. Any extra days and fittings you can allow will produce a better garment. Suits of Thai silk and Hong Kong ultra suede cost a fraction of ready-made items in the shops at home.

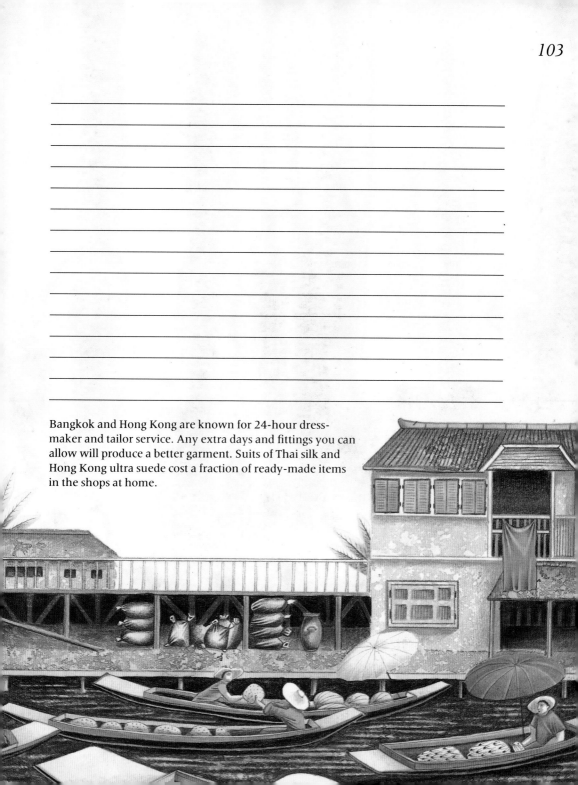

Sun in tropical countries and at great heights is incredibly strong, and the highest sun block available is a must, plus hat and sleeved shirt. Fair skinned children should use a high factor waterproof block on all exposed parts, and also wear T-shirts for bathing for at least half the day. Avoid too much sun between the hours of ten and two. Don't apply aftersun products until the skin has cooled down completely.

_____
_____
_____
_____
_____
_____
_____
_____
_____
_____
_____
_____
_____
_____
_____
_____
_____
_____
_____
_____
_____
_____

Lovers of the strange and dramatic should look for interesting islands rich in folklore or wildlife – Papua New Guinea, the Aran Islands off the west coast of Ireland, Belle Isle in Brittanny or Easter Island in the Pacific Ocean.

Duty-free shops are not always the bargain they appear to be. Amsterdam's Schipol is still one of the best. If you know the discount prices of electronics and cameras back home, you won't be misled.

_____

_____

_____

_____

_____

_____

_____

_____

_____

_____

_____

_____

_____

_____

Overweight charges can be one per cent of the first class fare per kilo, so it pays to pack lightly. Take no more than you can comfortably carry for fifteen minutes, as one frequent traveller advises.

When visiting central Australia or malaria-risk countries, arm yourself against mosquitos and flies by taking a veil as well as an insect repellant which contains 100% DEET. The danger is greatest in the evening hours.

To discourage thieves in Latin America and Africa, carry old, worn luggage with a good lock. Elegant luggage attracts thieves, even once you've checked it in for a flight. Avoid travelling with anything of value.

The best times for the most effective pictures are early morning or late afternoon, when shadows are long, and back lighting creates interesting silhouettes. Avoid the hours of twelve to three when the light is flat.

_____

_____

_____

_____

_____

_____

_____

_____

_____

_____

_____

_____

_____

_____

_____

_____

Select a theme for your holiday snapshots, such as doorways, windows, park benches, and make sure you include local people in your pictures. Don't be afraid to move in close to your subject.

Kenya's national parks are famous for antelope (Mara Masai Reserve), elephants (Tsavo National Park), rhinos (Amboseli Masai Reserve). Tanzania's Ngorongoro Crater is filled with zebra, lions, wildebeeste, buffaloes, elephants and rhinos, while the Serengeti National Park has a spectacular concentration of migratory game. Visit Kruger National Park in South Africa, one of the largest game reserves in the world, in winter and spring months when the grass is low.

When driving around Africa, be flexible about your itinerary. Border crossings are unreliable and liable to close at short notice. Keep plenty of fuel on board in case of a long and tedious detour.

_____
_____
_____
_____
_____
_____
_____
_____
_____
_____
_____
_____
_____
_____
_____
_____

If you enjoy your food, make notes about the meals you eat,
good wines, any interesting ingredients, or things to avoid
another time. If you come across any amusing English
translations of foreign dishes, you might note them here.

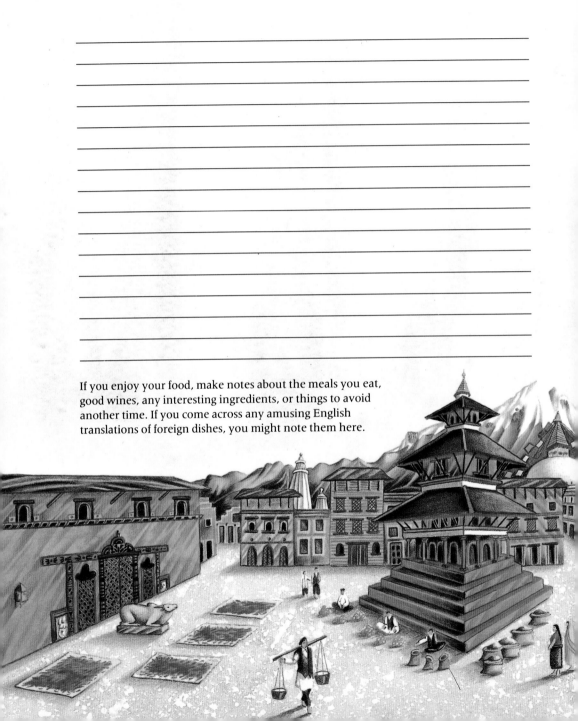

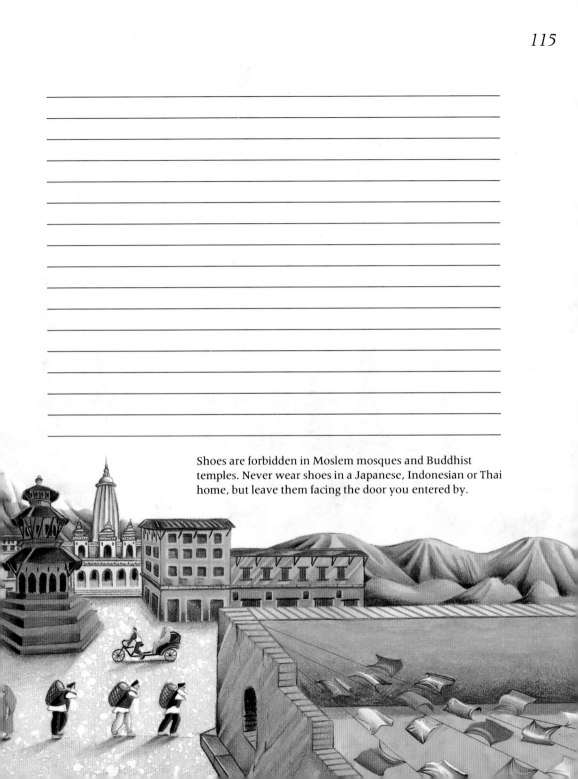

Shoes are forbidden in Moslem mosques and Buddhist temples. Never wear shoes in a Japanese, Indonesian or Thai home, but leave them facing the door you entered by.

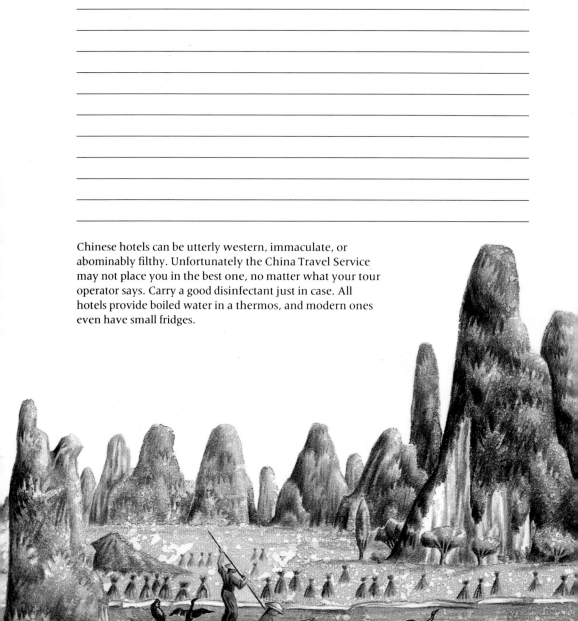

Chinese hotels can be utterly western, immaculate, or
abominably filthy. Unfortunately the China Travel Service
may not place you in the best one, no matter what your tour
operator says. Carry a good disinfectant just in case. All
hotels provide boiled water in a thermos, and modern ones
even have small fridges.

The Chinese collect personal luggage tags. Be safe, always put one inside your luggage, and place an uninteresting one on the outside.

_____

_____

_____

_____

_____

_____

_____

_____

_____

_____

_____

_____

_____

Keep toddlers amused by taking both familiar and new toys and games on long trips. Bring along a stuffed animal for bedtime. Young children love to draw with colourful felt tip pens. Make 'maps' by resting the pen on a pad of plain paper and letting the motion of the car or train joggle the hand randomly to make a pattern.

_____
_____
_____
_____
_____
_____
_____
_____
_____
_____
_____
_____
_____
_____
_____

Plan to use an unconventional means of transport on your
next holiday – perhaps a mailboat in the Bahamas, a llama
trek in Peru, a vintage luxury train in Spain, Russia or India,
a hot-air balloon in the Alps, or a donkey in the Greek
mountains and hills.

_____
_____
_____
_____
_____
_____
_____
_____
_____
_____
_____
_____
_____
_____
_____
_____
_____

Meeting foreigners is easiest if you are travelling alone. The
larger your party, the fewer locals you will meet. Split up
occasionally, and then join forces later to compare your
experiences.

_____
_____
_____
_____
_____
_____
_____
_____
_____
_____
_____
_____
_____
_____
_____
_____
_____

If two individuals or couples travel together, interests often clash. Plan to spend part of the day doing things separately, and get together for the evening meal.

Make a point of looking for the countryside hospitality on offer in Eastern Europe and New Zealand. In Britain, you can stay in old manor houses and stately homes as if you were in your own home.

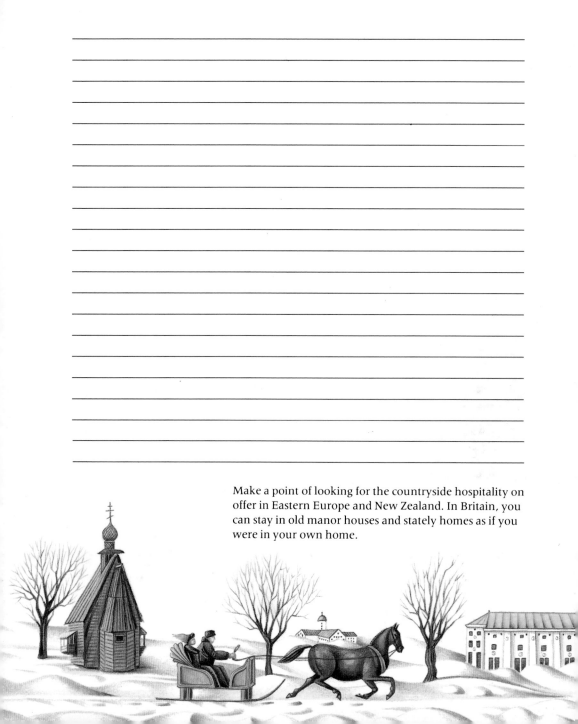

_____
_____
_____
_____
_____
_____
_____
_____
_____
_____
_____
_____
_____
_____
_____
_____
_____

For those who prefer self catering with a difference, there
are many restored landmarks such as a copper mine engine
house beside a stream in Cornwall or fortress buildings on
the South Wales coast.

Consider house swapping as a way of experiencing what it is like to live in another country. Although you will be staying in someone else's house, you may never actually meet the owners. You can be sure your home will be well cared for, as they hope you are doing the same for them.

_____
_____
_____
_____
_____
_____
_____
_____
_____
_____
_____
_____
_____
_____

It is easier for a thief to steal a handbag than a money belt.
Cotton ones are more comfortable than nylon or plastic.
Men should carry their wallets inside their jackets, never in
a back or side trouser pocket. Better still, use hotel safe
deposits, and carry little cash.

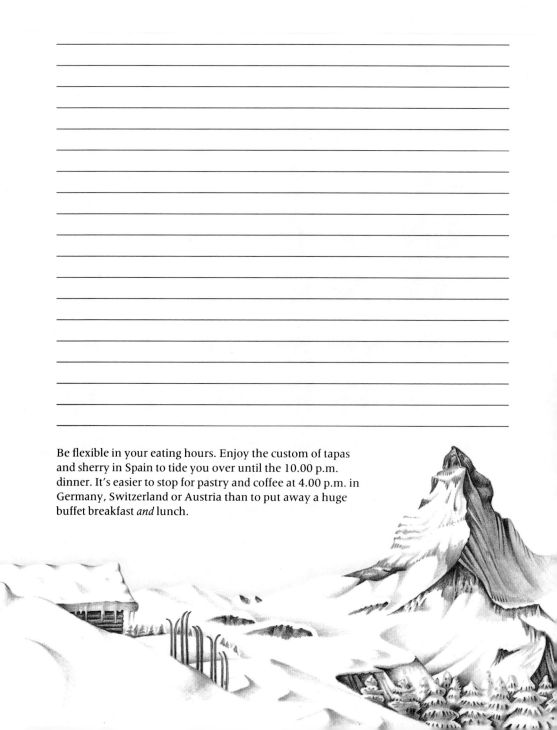

Be flexible in your eating hours. Enjoy the custom of tapas and sherry in Spain to tide you over until the 10.00 p.m. dinner. It's easier to stop for pastry and coffee at 4.00 p.m. in Germany, Switzerland or Austria than to put away a huge buffet breakfast *and* lunch.

A large lightweight scarf comes in useful in summer and winter. It protects against sunburn or drafts when driving, becomes a wrap for evening, and extends a basic holiday wardrobe.

How well do you know your own province/state/shire?
Imagine you must show a foreigner the wonders of your
own part of the world, and learn more about its scenic and
cultural offerings. Once you begin to look at things as a
visitor from abroad, you may find exquisite gardens,
fascinating museums, talented choirs, a Roman road,
interesting minorities.

_____
_____
_____
_____
_____
_____
_____
_____
_____
_____
_____

A present is always appreciated, especially something you've brought from your own country. Whatever you offer in Japan, it should be beautifully wrapped. When invited to dinner, flowers are always a safe gesture, but do avoid red roses in Germany or Switzerland, unless you have romantic aspirations. In Germany, a man should unwrap flowers before presenting them to a lady.

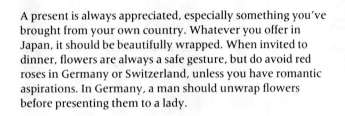

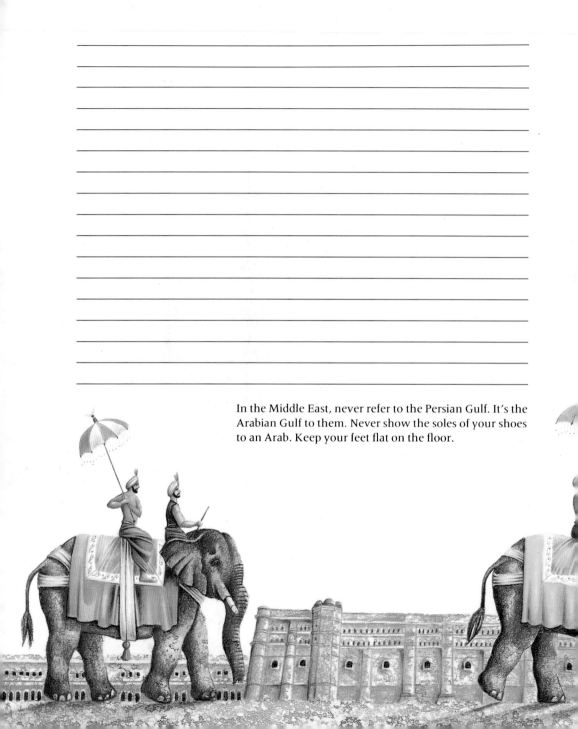

In the Middle East, never refer to the Persian Gulf. It's the Arabian Gulf to them. Never show the soles of your shoes to an Arab. Keep your feet flat on the floor.

Out of respect, refrain from eye contact in India. A red dot on the forehead usually means a woman is married. Men and women don't touch each other, or shake hands. A slight bow, with your palms together, is appropriate.

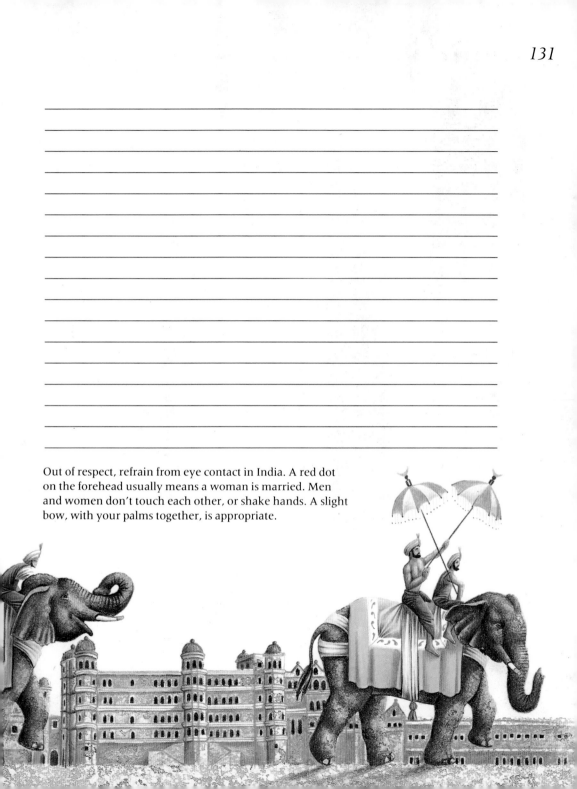

T.I.P. means To Insure Promptness. Tip at the beginning of a long stay, rather than at the end. Americans usually overtip when abroad because they are unaccustomed to inclusive service charges. Find out the local custom before checking into a hotel. Hard currency is greatly appreciated by cab drivers, concierges, and porters in poorer countries.

_____

_____

_____

_____

_____

_____

_____

_____

_____

_____

_____

_____

_____

_____

_____

_____

_____

_____

_____

For quick refunds, the best travellers cheques are Barclays Visa, Thomas Cook, American Express, and Citibank, or those issued by German and Swiss banks. Get cheques denominated in US dollars for travel in the US, where they can be used as cash everywhere. Get cheques in French francs for travel to West African countries whose currency (the CFA) is pegged to the franc.

Rules on picnicing or camping inside national parks in the US are very strict. Special areas are set aside and only these can be used. Use the grills and litterbins provided. It is a serious crime to remove anything from the park, such as pieces of attractive rock, flowers or pieces of wood. In some parks inspections are made of car boots (trunks) as you leave the area – a bit like going through customs!

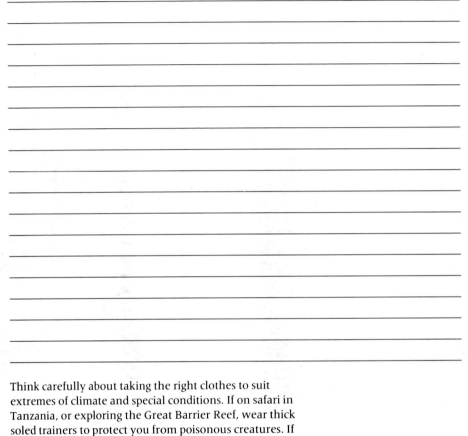

Think carefully about taking the right clothes to suit extremes of climate and special conditions. If on safari in Tanzania, or exploring the Great Barrier Reef, wear thick soled trainers to protect you from poisonous creatures. If necessary, get expert advice.

_____

_____

_____

_____

_____

_____

_____

_____

_____

_____

_____

_____

_____

_____

_____

_____

If no-one is looking after your home in your absence,
consider having the Post Office hold or forward your mail.
They will do it for as little as a week, or up to twelve months.
Give them a week's notice.

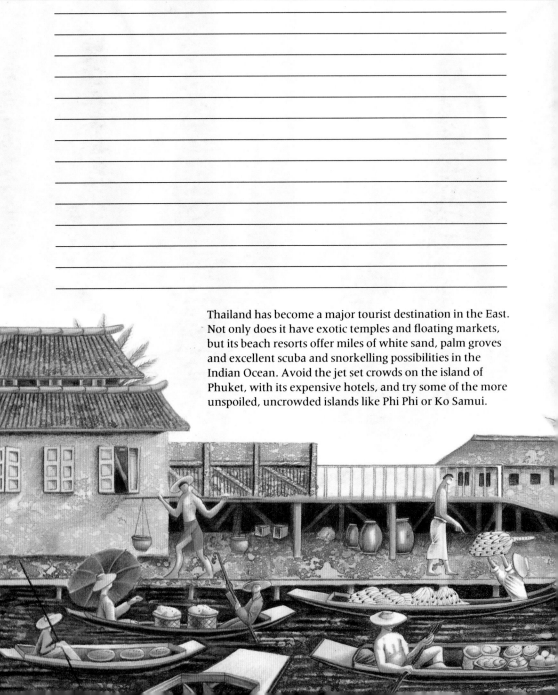

Thailand has become a major tourist destination in the East. Not only does it have exotic temples and floating markets, but its beach resorts offer miles of white sand, palm groves and excellent scuba and snorkelling possibilities in the Indian Ocean. Avoid the jet set crowds on the island of Phuket, with its expensive hotels, and try some of the more unspoiled, uncrowded islands like Phi Phi or Ko Samui.

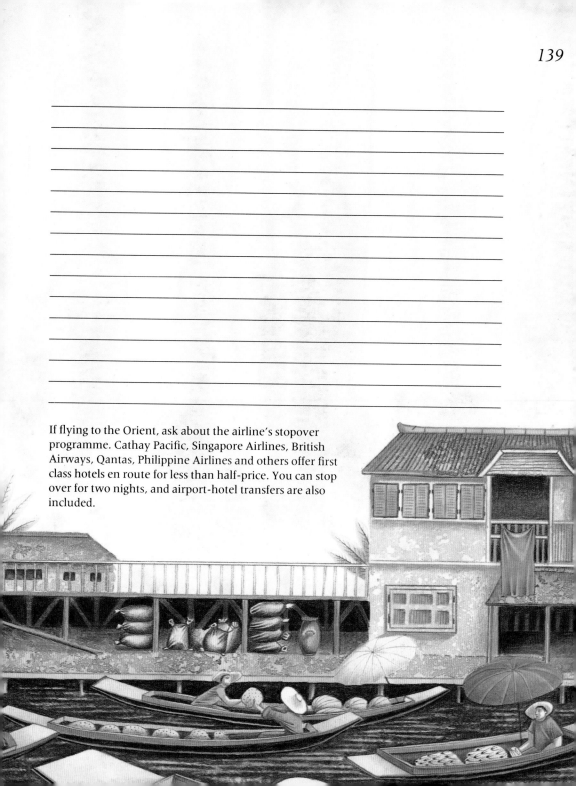

_____

_____

_____

_____

_____

_____

_____

_____

_____

_____

_____

_____

_____

If flying to the Orient, ask about the airline's stopover
programme. Cathay Pacific, Singapore Airlines, British
Airways, Qantas, Philippine Airlines and others offer first
class hotels en route for less than half-price. You can stop
over for two nights, and airport-hotel transfers are also
included.

_____
_____
_____
_____
_____
_____
_____
_____
_____
_____
_____
_____
_____

Indonesia is an ideal place for a holiday because of the multitude of cultural things on offer – dance, puppets, arts and crafts, textiles, ancient buildings. There are beautiful beaches, spectacular rice terraces, friendly people, comfortable places to stay and it is easy to travel about. It pays to be adventurous and to get off the beaten track, but bus journeys can be strenuous. While the jungle is alive with monkeys, they can be vicious and grab food from your hands.

To get rid of creases, turn on the hot water in the shower. When the bathroom is steamy, hang the garment up, and leave it there for ten minutes. Remove from the bathroom, and let it dry for thirty minutes before wearing. Pack your own non-rusty hangers; you will find there are never enough in hotel rooms.

_____

_____

_____

_____

_____

_____

_____

_____

_____

_____

_____

_____

_____

_____

_____

_____

_____

_____

_____

_____

Have you found any amusing notices on your journey such
as the one seen in an Italian cleaners: 'Ladies, leave your
clothes here and spend the afternoon having a good time', or
in a distant airport: 'We take your bags and send them in all
directions'?

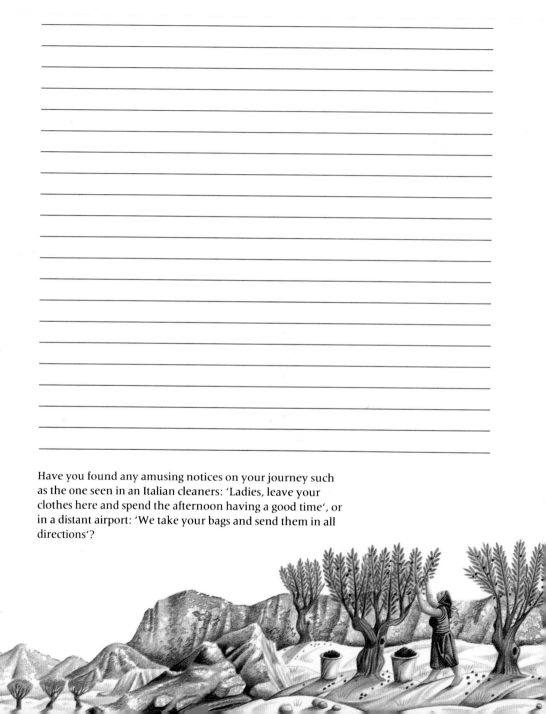

_____
_____
_____
_____
_____
_____
_____
_____
_____
_____
_____
_____
_____
_____

Keep a page or two of this diary to note down linguistic
expressions, either just the basics so that you can get by, or
some special phrases with which to impress people or which
are not in the dictionary. Get the prices written down when
you don't understand.

Get a reservation at the small Machu Picchu hotel in order
to enjoy Peru's Inca site without hoards of tourists. Climb
Huayna Picchu at sunrise, but bring good rubber-soled
shoes, as the narrow path is slippery.

_____

_____

_____

_____

_____

_____

_____

_____

_____

_____

_____

_____

_____

_____

_____

_____

_____

The Cuzco-Machu Picchu train passes some of the world's
most lush scenery, including the dashing Urubamba River.
Reserve seats in the tourist car if you don't want to travel
with the chickens and natives.

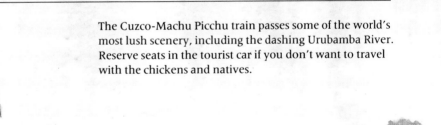

FACT FILE

As a ready source of reference, here is some information which has proved useful over the years. If you wish, you may clip in and add other material to this section: plane seating guides, train schedules, vintage charts. Some people may choose to photocopy their favourite maps, and track their route to keep as an extra record.

If you need more space for extra statistics, simply use some of the blank pages from the *Holiday Diary* section. Some travellers like to make currency conversion tables or to note mileages.

The very last pages are for you to fill in your own *Vital Information*. It is handy to have certain personal details on one page while travelling, and it could be invaluable in case of an emergency. But be sure to complete this page before setting out on your journey, and add further details as you go.

Time Zones

1.00	2.00	3.00	4.00	5.00	6.00	7.00	8.00	9.00	10.00	11

Midday in Leningrad is midnight in Tahiti. In other words, at the point of the earth directly under the sun it is midday, while at the opposite end it is midnight. In 1884 an international convention mapped out the twenty four time zones shown here. Times are based on Greenwich Mean Time. This chart will help you to work out the time in the different places you are visiting. Remember to check whether there is one standard time countrywide, and whether there is daylight saving (summer time). Use this page when ringing home, but be sure to check what the time is at the other end when you make the call!

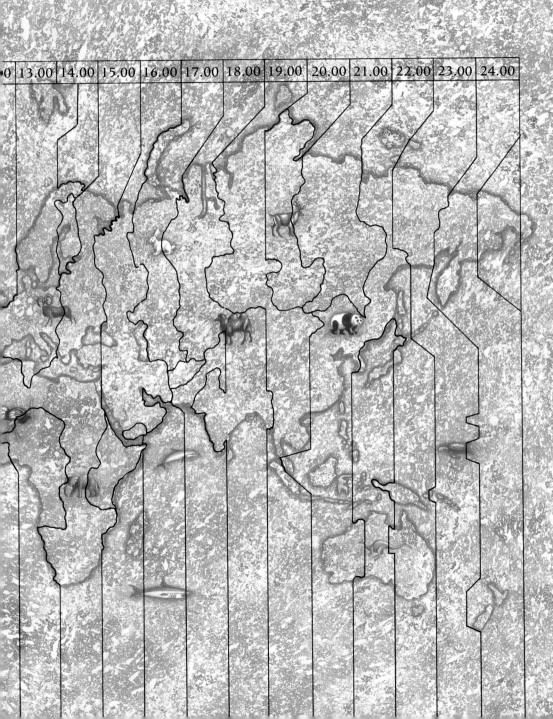

Best Weather Guide

Weather can make or break a holiday. Here is a list of what are considered to be the most pleasant times of year to visit favourite holiday destinations. It will help you to plan where to go, and when to make a trip. Travel agents can provide further information. The temperatures listed in tour operators' brochures are generally taken at noon in the shade. The hottest time of day is normally early afternoon. Remember to make allowances for location, altitude and prevailing winds.

NORTH AMERICA

NEW YORK	JUNE, SEPTEMBER, OCTOBER
NEW ORLEANS	MARCH, APRIL
MIAMI	NOVEMBER TO APRIL
BAHAMAS	DECEMBER TO APRIL
ROCKY MOUNTAINS	JULY, AUGUST
SAN FRANCISCO	APRIL TO NOVEMBER
ALASKA	JULY, AUGUST
NEW ENGLAND	JUNE TO OCTOBER
VANCOUVER	MAY TO SEPTEMBER
WASHINGTON	APRIL TO JUNE

CENTRAL/SOUTH AMERICA

MEXICO	NOVEMBER TO APRIL
ARGENTINA	JUNE TO OCTOBER
RIO	MAY TO SEPTEMBER

MIDDLE EAST

ISRAEL	APRIL TO JUNE, SEPTEMBER TO NOVEMBER
U.A.E.	DECEMBER, JANUARY, APRIL TO JUNE

AFRICA

SOUTH AFRICA	APRIL, MAY, SEPTEMBER
KENYA	DECEMBER TO MARCH
EGYPT	OCTOBER TO APRIL
TUNISIA	APRIL TO JUNE, SEPTEMBER TO NOVEMBER
SEYCHELLES	JULY, AUGUST

SOUTH PACIFIC/ASIA

HONG KONG	OCTOBER TO MARCH
TAHITI	JUNE TO OCTOBER
SYDNEY	JANUARY TO MAY
WELLINGTON	JANUARY TO MARCH
THAILAND	NOVEMBER TO JANUARY
JAPAN	SPRING AND AUTUMN
PHILIPPINES	NOVEMBER TO MARCH

SUB CONTINENT

INDIA	OCTOBER TO MARCH
NEPAL	MARCH, OCTOBER TO DECEMBER
SRI LANKA	FEBRUARY TO APRIL, AUGUST TO NOVEMBER

EUROPE

GREECE	MAY, JUNE, SEPTEMBER
TURKEY	MAY TO OCTOBER
CYPRUS	MARCH TO NOVEMBER
YUGOSLAVIA	JUNE TO SEPTEMBER
MALTA	MARCH TO OCTOBER
SCANDINAVIA	MAY TO JULY
USSR	MAY TO SEPTEMBER

Festivals and Special Events

Festivals can give a good insight into a country's soul and
way of life. Listed here are some of the more interesting
annual festivals worldwide. Only the months are indicated,
so check precise dates each year with tourist offices. You will
find plenty more local events when you reach your
destination. Some people will find this list a helpful
indication of the places to avoid at certain times of year.

JANUARY	THE SYDNEY FESTIVAL, AUSTRALIA
	THE GREAT QUEENSTOWN GOLD RUSH
	ROBERT BURNS NIGHT, SCOTLAND
	VIKING BOAT-BURNING CEREMONY, SHETLANDS
	TASMANIA SURF CHAMPIONSHIPS, AUSTRALIA
FEBRUARY	CARNIVAL IN VENICE, RIO, VIENNA, COLOGNE, NICE,
	MARDI GRAS, NEW ORLEANS, USA
	CHIANG MAI FLOWER FESTIVAL, THAILAND
	LOULE CARNIVAL, PORTUGAL
	CHINESE NEW YEAR
	FASTNACHT, BASEL, SWITZERLAND
MARCH/	EASTER/HOLY WEEK IN SPAIN, ESP. SEVILLE
APRIL	EASTER/ORTHODOX CELEBRATIONS IN GREEK
	VILLAGES
	CHERRY BLOSSOM FESTIVAL, WASHINGTON, DC
APRIL	SECHSILAUTEN SPRING FESTIVAL, ZURICH
	LANDSGEMEINDE, APPENZELL, SWITZERLAND

APRIL	CHERRY BLOSSOM TIME, JAPAN
	KENTUCKY DERBY, LOUISVILLE, KENTUCKY
	FERIA, SEVILLE
	LONDON MARATHON
	MADEIRA FLOWER FESTIVAL, PORTUGAL

MAY	LABOUR DAY PARADE, MOSCOW
	ASCENSION DAY PROCESSION, BRUGES
	GRAND PRIX, MONACO, MONTE CARLO
	CANNES FILM FESTIVAL
	WINDMILL DAY, HOLLAND
	CAT FESTIVAL, YPRES, BELGIUM
	GLYNDEBOURNE FESTIVAL BEGINS, ENGLAND
	CHELSEA FLOWER SHOW, LONDON
	SAGRA DE SANT EFISIO PROCESSION, CAGLIARI, SARDINIA
	VIENNA FESTIVAL BEGINS, AUSTRIA

JUNE	MID-SUMMER FESTIVAL, SWEDEN
	PARIS AIR SHOW, LE BOURGET
	ALDEBURGH FESTIVAL, SUFFOLK
	LE MANS RACE, FRANCE
	INTERNATIONAL DRAGON BOAT RACES, HONG KONG
	ASCOT RACES/WIMBLEDON WEEK, ENGLAND
	WHITE NIGHTS FESTIVAL, LENINGRAD

| JULY | TOUR DE FRANCE BICYCLE RACE |
| | VERONA OPERA FESTIVAL BEINGS, ITALY |

JULY	PALIO HORSE RACE AND PARADE, SIENA
	BASTILLE DAY, FRANCE
	SAN FERMIN FESTIVAL, PAMPLONA
	CALGARY STAMPEDE, ALBERTA, CANADA
	IL REDENTORE GONDOLA PROCESSION, VENICE
	WAGNER FESTIVAL BEGINS, BAYREUTH
	SALZBURG FESTIVAL BEGINS, AUSTRIA
	BREGENZ FESTIVAL BEINGS, AUSTRIA
	OMMEGANG FOLKLORE PAGEANT, BRUSSELS
	SAVONLINNA OPERA FESTIVAL, FINLAND
	ESTORIL MUSIC FESTIVAL BEGINS, PORTUGAL
	DUBROVNIK FESTIVAL BEGINS, YUGOSLAVIA
	AVIGNON FESTIVAL BEGINS, FRANCE
AUGUST	DUBLIN HORSE SHOW, IRELAND
	EDINBURGH FESTIVAL AND FRINGE BEGINS
SEPTEMBER	HIGHLAND GAMES, BRAEMAR, SCOTLAND
	VENICE REGATTA, ITALY
	ALOHA WEEK, HONOLULU
	ARHUS FESTIVAL, DENMARK
	MONTEREY JAZZ FESTIVAL, CALIFORNIA
	GREVENMACHER WINE FESTIVAL, LUXEMBOURG
	BATTLE OF THE FLOWERS, LARERO, SPAIN
	INTERNATIONAL OYSTER FESTIVAL, GALWAY
	DUBLIN THEATRE FESTIVAL BEGINS
	FIESTA DE LA MERCED, BARCELONA
	OKTOBERFEST BEGINS, MUNICH

OCTOBER	*TIGER FISH COMPETITION, ZIMBABWE*
	WEXFORD OPERA FESTIVAL, IRELAND
NOVEMBER	*NEW YORK MARATHON*
	MELBOURNE CUP, AUSTRALIA
	AUSTRALIAN GRAND PRIX, ADELAIDE
	PUSKAR GAME FAIR, RAJASTHAN, INDIA
	ELEPHANT HURD-UP, SURIN, THAILAND
DECEMBER	*CHRISTMAS MARKETS IN GERMANY AND AUSTRIA*
	LUCIA FESTIVAL, SWEDEN
	NEW YEAR'S EVE IN FUNCHAL, MADEIRA
	ST NIKOLAUS DAY, INNSBRUCK
	JUNKANCO FESTIVAL, BAHAMAS

Conversion Tables

Here are some conversion tables which you may find useful while you are on holiday, particularly when you are shopping. The tables giving clothes and shoe sizes are just an approximate guide. Sizes and fittings will vary from country to country and from manufacturer to manufacturer. Always try on the items before making a purchase. To convert Fahrenheit to Celsius, subtract 32, multiply by 5 and divide by 9. To convert Celsius to Fahrenheit, multiply by 9, divide by 5 and add 32.

FAHRENHEIT – CELSIUS

−10	−23.33	46	7.78	84	28.89
−6	−21.11	54	12.22	88	31.11
0	−17.78	60	15.56	92	33.33
+10	−12.22	66	18.89	98	36.67
+20	−6.67	70	21.11	102	38.89
+32	0	74	23.33	106	41.11
40	+4.44	80	26.67	212	100

CELSIUS – FAHRENHEIT

−32	−25.6	14	57.2	30	86
−20	−4	18	64.4	34	93.2
−14	+6.8	20	68	36	96.8
−10	+14	22	71.6	38	100.4
−4	+24.8	24	75.2	40	104
+2	35.6	26	78.8	42	107.6
10	50	28	82.4	100	212

WEIGHTS

1 GRAM	.035 OUNCE
100 GRAMS	3.527 OUNCES
1 KILOGRAM	2.205 POUNDS
1 TONNE	1.1 TONS
1 OUNCE	28.35 GRAMS
1 POUND	0.45 KILOGRAM

LIQUID

1 MILLILITRE	0.03 FL OUNCE
1 LITRE	2.1 PINTS
1 LITRE	0.26 GALLON
1 CUP	0.24 LITRE
1 PINT	0.47 LITRE
1 GALLON	3.8 LITRES

LENGTH

1 MILLIMETRE	0.039 INCH
1 CENTIMETRE	0.39 INCH
1 METRE	39.37 INCHES/1.1 YARDS
1 KILOMETRE	.62 MILE
1 INCH	2.54 CENTIMETRES
1 FOOT	30 CENTIMETRES
1 YARD	0.9 METRE
1 MILE	1.6 KILOMETRES

SURFACE

1 SQ CENTIMETRE	0.16 SQ INCH
1 SQ METRE	1.197 SQ YARDS
1 SQ KILOMETRE	.386 SQ MILE
1 HECTARE	2.47 ACRES
1 SQ INCH	6.5 SQ CENTIMETRES
1 SQ FOOT	0.09 SQ METRE
1 SQ YARD	0.8 SQ METRE
1 ACRE	0.4 HECTARE

CLOTHES SIZES

MEN'S SUITS

US	36	38	39	41	42	44	45	47	48
BRITISH	36	38	39	41	42	44	45	47	48
CONTINENTAL	46	48	50	52	54	56	58	60	62

MEN'S SHIRTS

US	$14^1/_2$	15	$15^1/_2$	16	$16^1/_2$	17	$17^1/_2$	18
BRITISH	$14^1/_2$	15	$15^1/_2$	16	$16^1/_2$	17	$17^1/_2$	18
CONTINENTAL	36	38	39	41	42	44	45	46

WOMEN'S COATS, DRESSES, SUITS

US	6	8	10	12	14	16	18
BRITISH	8	10	12	14	16	18	20
CONTINENTAL	34	38	40	42	44	46	48

WOMEN'S BLOUSES, SWEATERS

US	8	10	12	14	16	18	20
BRITISH	32	34	36	38	40	42	44
CONTINENTAL	38	40	42	44	46	48	50

CHILDREN

US	3	4	5	6	6X
BRITISH	18	20	22	24	26
CONTINENTAL	98	104	110	116	122

SHOES

US WOMEN	$4^1/_2$	$5^1/_2$	$6^1/_2$	$7^1/_2$	$8^1/_2$	$9^1/_2$	$10^1/_2$	$11^1/_2$	$12^1/_2$	$13^1/_2$	$14^1/_2$
US MEN	–	–	$5^1/_2$	$6^1/_2$	$7^1/_2$	$8^1/_2$	$9^1/_2$	$10^1/_2$	$11^1/_2$	$12^1/_2$	$13^1/_2$
BRITISH	3	4	5	6	7	8	9	10	11	12	13
CONTINENTAL	36	37	38	39	40	42	43	44	45	47	48

Voltage Guide

If you take an electric razor, hair dryer, or iron with you,
don't forget adaptors and plugs, and make sure that you
change your appliance to the right voltage. For a safe
holiday, check what is correct, particularly in those countries
where there are variations.

110 VOLTS

COLOMBIA, CUBA, JAPAN, MAJORCA, PANAMA, USA, VIRGIN ISLANDS

110/220 VOLTS

ALGERIA, ANTIGUA, BAHAMAS, BARBADOS, BELGIUM, BERMUDA,
BOLIVIA, BRAZIL, BULGARIA, CANADA, CANARY ISLANDS, COSTA
RICA, CZECHOSLOVAKIA, EGYPT, FRANCE, GERMANY, GREECE,
GUATEMALA, INDONESIA, ITALY, JAMAICA, LEBANON,
LUXEMBOURG, MALAYSIA, MARTINIQUE, MEXICO, MONACO,
MOROCCO, NETHERLANDS, PHILIPPINES, PORTUGAL, ROMANIA SAUDI
ARABIA, SINGAPORE, SPAIN, SWEDEN, SWITZERLAND, TAHITI,
TAIWAN, TRINIDAD AND TOBAGO, TUNISIA, TURKEY, USSR

220 VOLTS

ARGENTINA, AUSTRALIA, AUSTRIA, BAHRAIN, BANGLADESH,
BOTSWANA, BURMA, CHANNEL ISLANDS, CHINA, CYPRUS, DENMARK,
FINLAND, GAMBIA, GIBRALTAR, GHANA, HONG KONG, HUNGARY,
ICELAND, INDIA, IRAN, IRAQ, IRELAND, ISRAEL, JORDAN, KENYA,
S. KOREA, KUWAIT, LIECHTENSTEIN, MADEIRA, MALAWI, MALTA,
NEPAL, NEW ZEALAND, NIGERIA, NORWAY, OMAN, PAKISTAN, PAPUA
NEW GUINEA, PARAGUAY, PERU, SEYCHELLES, SIERRA LEONE,
SOUTH AFRICA, SRI LANKA, TANZANIA, UGANDA, URUGUAY, UNITED
ARAB EMIRATES, UNITED KINGDOM, YUGOSLAVIA. ZAMBIA,
ZIMBABWE

Vital Information

Keep all personal information and critical telephone
numbers in one place. You may wish to refer to it in the
course of your vacation. Prepare yourself for unforeseen
difficulties and emergencies by filling in this page in
advance. If your important papers are separated from you, it
will be helpful to have all the details to hand. Make a list of
(and maybe photograph) all your valuables and relevant
serial numbers. Never put these items in your checked
luggage – keep them with you. Take photocopies of
important documents.

PASSPORT: NUMBER   EXPIRY DATE
_____

PLACE/DATE OF ISSUE
_____

VISA NUMBERS AND EXPIRY DATES
_____

TELEPHONE NUMBERS:
_____
RELATIVE
_____
LAWYER
_____
TRAVEL AGENT
_____
EMBASSY/CONSULATE
_____
LOCAL DOCTOR
_____
     DENTIST
_____
     PHARMACY
_____
OTHER
_____
_____
_____
_____
_____
_____

BANK _____ ACCOUNT NUMBER _____

CREDIT CARD/S _____ CARD NUMBER/S _____

_____

_____

_____

_____

TRAVELLERS CHEQUES ____ CHEQUE NUMBERS _____
EMERGENCY NUMBER _____

DRIVING LICENSE NUMBER _____
AIRLINE TICKET NUMBER _____
SERIAL NUMBERS OF VALUABLES _____

_____

OTHER _____

_____

_____

_____

_____

_____

_____

_____

_____

_____

Addresses and Telephone Numbers

NAME	ADDRESS	TELEPHONE

NAME	ADDRESS	TELEPHONE

OTHER TITLES IN THIS SERIES FROM EYEBRIGHT

OUR GARDEN BOOK
The Garden Planner and Record Keeper
£8.95   ISBN 0 948751 01 0

OUR HOUSE BOOK
The Home Record Keeper
£8.95   ISBN 0 948751 00 2

RECIPES
A Notebook for Cooks
£8.95   ISBN 0 948751 02 9

PRESENTS
A Gift Record Book
£8.95   ISBN 0 948751 03 7

ORDER FORM

Note: If you don't want to spoil your book, make a photocopy of this coupon instead.

Please send me _____ copies of OUR HOUSE BOOK @ £10.50 including post and packing

Please send me _____ copies of OUR GARDEN BOOK @ £10.50 including post and packing

Please send me _____ copies of RECIPES @ £10.50 including post and packing

Please send me _____ copies of PRESENTS @ £10.5O including post and packing

I enclose a cheque for a total of _____ made payable to Eyebright Publications at the following address: 21 Weedon Lane, Amersham, Bucks HP6 5QT. Allow 28 days for delivery.

Name _____

Address _____

_____ Post Code _____

Regarding corporate or deluxe editions of this book, please call Eyebright Publications on 081 348 4997